Songs of Love and Grammar

Songs of Love and Grammar

by James Harbeck
illustrations by Jonathan Lu

ISBN 978-1-105-61733-1

www.lulu.com

Contents

Unromantic interlude (not about love etc.)

X-rated! (not for sensitive eyes)

R-rated (adult, but not quite as sizzling)

For Aina, who puts up with me every day.
And thanks to whom I am free from the stresses of
romantic uncertainty.

—*James Harbeck*

James Harbeck

G-rated (sweet and safe for all audiences)

Shall I compare you...

Shall I compare you to a semi-colon,
a pause, a dot, a stroke, a sideways wink?
Have you become a half-stop lightly fallen
upon my page in form of dots of ink?

Or are you more a comma, little pause,
not semi-colon – only one dot now
to separate a modifying clause,
a flick, a swish, a little pixie's bow?

Perhaps you jump out as an exclamation,
a point, a shock, a look-at-me-will-you.
Perhaps a cool regard's your inclination –
you tuck your tail and make a colon true.

Oh, let me try you; let me count the ways
that I may fit you into my life's phrase.

Dashing around

*M*y boyfriend is the dashing type.
He writes – whips off – with vim – and hype.
He goes – he comes – cycle completing –
and yet – I feel – he may be cheating.
Last week he sent a note – "Dear N –
I hope – so soon – we join – again!"
But then – missent – another too –
"Dear M—can't wait—to meet—with you!"
From N – to M—his life's a whirl!
He's dashing—yes – from girl to girl!
I think I should have picked a man
with more breath & attention span.
I'll find & marry someone bland
who'll come & stay with ampersand.

Dashes are sentence punctuation, used to join - or separate - phrases, whereas hyphens are word punctuation. There are two main types of dash (though they're not the only ones out there): the en-dash, -, so called because it's as wide as an **n**, and the em-dash, —, which is as wide as an **m**. The em-dash is used to separate phrases, not unlike a semicolon, or to set off a parenthetical comment (rather than using parentheses or commas), but it can also be used where a colon would be, or to conjoin disjoint thoughts. It usually does not have a space on either side. The en-dash is used to express such things as number ranges, e.g., **consumers 25–35 years old**, but it can also be in place of the em-dash in a sentence, with a space on either side. Oh, and the ampersand? See next...

Written in the stars

*A*s everybody knows, I like to write,
but there are some who shun what I have written
and think my keyboard should be dynamitten
for lines that others think are dynamite.

One winter day, an email full of spite
rejecting poetry to me was spitten.
The editor was not so eruditten,
but said *my* words should be more erudite.

I felt he had just said it to incite.
I stomped out – to fresh air I felt incitten!
I slammed the door. My eaves were stalactitten,
and I was nearly speared by stalactite.

'Twas deepest winter; all the world was white.
I saw a pretty girl with fingers whitten,
and so I doffed and offered her a mitten
and asked if she would dine with me a mite.

I know not where my nerve came to invite
this lovely apparition, but, invitten,
she acquiesced, and soon we both were sitten
at table in a food and beverage site.

Then Cupid pulled his arrow labelled "smite,"
and pretty girl and I were tandem smitten.
'Twas obvious to all we both were bitten
by love before we'd even had a bite.

Her skin, her eyes, her words, did all excite,
and by me she, too, somehow was excitten.
From then, at every chance, we were unitten,
and soon a minister did us unite.

Now all my verse I first to her recite.
As to the story I've above recitten,
I'm happy for the note that had me quitten
my home – but for the sentiment, not quite.

I haven't changed the style that I indite,
but many read and buy what I've inditten.
And so to those who'd drown my inner kitten,
all I have to say is: Fly a kite.

The -en endings for past participles come down from a class of verbs in Old English. This isn't a serious disquisition on them, of course. I actually wrote it just so I could say the last two lines. Remember: just because someone is po-faced doesn't mean he or she is right.

I love; I despair

The semicolon: a great divide;
it tears my heart right up inside.
It is my treasure; my delight;
my comfort morning, noon, and night;
a present help in time of need;
a means to make syntax succeed.
It is like ink-spot wedding rings;
it joins two independent things.
It saves my mind from apoplexity
when faced with lists of great complexity.
And yet, how can I sing my song
when all around me it's used wrong?
I have received an amorous note
that rends my spirit just to quote:
"I worship you for reasons two;
all that you are; all that you do.
I write to make you this proposal;
life to spend at your disposal.
My upshot is; it's plain to see;
I'm asking you to; marry me."
Now I am faced with choice so stark
twixt love and punctuation mark.
How can I live when I have fallen
for a butcher of the semicolon?

I confess: misuse of semicolons drives me crazy. It's properly used to join list items when they have punctuation within them, and to join two syntactically independent but thematically joined phrases – in other words, it's a period that doesn't want to be quite so definite. It can't replace a colon or, except in lists, a comma. And it doesn't make text look smarter when it's misused!

Joined by fate by April

Last fall I was hit by a stop sign
by a truck that failed to stop;
the driver was caught by a red light
and sent off to jail by a cop.
I was taken away by an ambulance
and laid by a nurse in a bed
in a hospital built by a river
and by morning was back from the dead.
I was kept in a room by the river
by the nurse to heal and stay.
I was seen by my bed by the window
by the nurse twice every day.
I was healed by the power of beauty:
I was struck by the nurse's face
and blown away by her lovely lips
by the time I left that place.
The nurse was known by April
by friends and by people about
and, by George, she was called by the next month
by me to ask her out.
By April she had been courted
by me for half a year
and by then it was time for a ring
to be given by me to my dear.
We were wed by a tree by a lake
by a hill by the moon by a priest
and the joining by God was feted
by the stars by our friends by a feast.
Now I'm joined in my life by April
and by fate we will never be parted,
and my wall is bedecked by the stop sign
by which this all was started.
By the wall a cradle's been placed,
and by April all will know why:
by and large, my April's grown pregnant,
and we'll have a child by and by.

The passive voice, aside from making a sentence less direct, can result in ambiguity thanks to that much-used preposition **by**. However, the passive voice isn't always the wrong thing to use - sometimes it allows for better flow. In which of the above sentences, if any, the passive is more useful than the active would be is left as an exercise to the reader. (!)

Signs of things to come

The @ has such a startled shape,
like an eye popped in surprise,
a clenching fist in terror bent,
or a mouth aghast, agape –
reminiscent of the look
you take on when you realize
the naughty email you just sent
went out to your whole address book.

The question mark is hooked in doubt
like a finger, beckoning,
or an eyebrow, in reaction
to that email you sent out.
The exclamation mark is rigid
like the rod of reckoning –
or a spine, when an attraction,
due to misplaced words, turns frigid.

You'll see the # sign some place
where cartoon artists stylize
someone running like a shot
or a bruise upon a face;
you'll find it on a telephone
when calling to apologize –
but emails sent cannot be caught...
you'll have to nurse your wounds alone.

For the rhythm to work, you need to read # **sign** as "number sign," not as
"pound sign" (which is not really a correct term for it). Alternately, you could
say "octothorpe" in place of "number sign." I decided to spell out **?** and **!**
because the odds of their being read as intended on the first pass didn't seem
high enough. Oh, and **@** is "at" here, nothing fancier.

Misplaced apprehensions

Yesterday evening, dressing to go out,
my wife and I shared a sense of doubt.
Putting on her lipstick, I told my dear
that somehow something wasn't clear.
Putting on my shirt, my wife told me
that she, too, felt uncertainty.
Pulling on her stockings, I asked my spouse
if anything was wrong within our house.
Tying on my tie, she told me again
that the cause of the trouble wasn't plain.
Pulling on a lovely satin gown,
I told her this was getting me down.
But then, in an insight, donning my jacket,
she told me she knew how to attack it.
She told me everything might be clearer
if we saw our reflections in the mirror.
Indeed, as we looked, we both were faced
with all the modifiers we'd misplaced:
Her lipstick, stockings, and gown wore I;
she had my jacket, shirt, and tie.
Swapping our clothes back helped us relax
and be more careful with our syntax.

It's actually quite common in English to use a modifier such as **putting on her lipstick** to refer not to the subject of the sentence, seen immediately following the modifier, but to the direct or indirect object or even just to a person (or thing) mentioned in the previous sentence. And often enough the reader can figure out who or what it's referring to. However, this construction – often referred to as a misplaced modifier – is best avoided, because it can create ambiguities – and because even when it doesn't create ambiguities, it can still make the sentence feel awkward, and may make the reader snicker a bit.

An apostrophe to a doomed romance

I met a guy who aimed to please.
At first, we seemed a perfect match,
but soon I found a little catch:
he overused apostrophes.

We'd go on date's; he'd buy me flower's;
he'd send me card's and write me rhyme's;
but, though we spent some lovely time's,
too soon his strokes wore on my hours.

Although his feeling's were impressive,
I thought of all the word's he'd had
and feared contracting something bad –
and felt that he was too possessive.

My lover plumbed my discontent.
He asked, "Why should a bit of ink
push heart's and spirit's to the brink?"
But when he said "Plea's stay," I went.

Apostrophes are meant to be used to indicate contractions (letters left out, as in **can't**) and possessives, and can be used for plurals only where they could otherwise be ambiguous ("My letter set is missing two a's"). There's no good reason to use them for any other plurals. Actually, we could get by without them almost entirely – you can't hear them when you're speaking, after all – but, ah, tradition.

Oh, and speaking of using them in contractions...

The gravitastrophe

for Carolyn Bishop

*H*ad I it in my pow'r
e'en for a wond'rous hour
to let words solemn hark'd
in print be plainly mark'd,
the mark I'd use would be
the gravitastrophe!

Momentous situations
oft call for syncopations;
howe'er, a plain contraction
is plebeian detraction.
To keep solemnity,
use gravitastrophe!

Take ink plash'd from a fount
on 'Lympus' heavn'ly mount;
'scribe it with quill-pen gain'd
from phoenix wing detain'd;
'gainst alabaster be
writ gravitastrophe!

Like cherub's down, the curl
shall clockwise-turn'd unfurl
'til, widdershins returning
(profan'd convention spurning),
with circlet tipp'd shall be
the gravitastrophe!

This stroke shall through the ages
be 'grav'd on scepter'd pages
so humbl'd reader knows
that whilom mundane prose
is rebirth'd poesy
with gravitastrophe!

My friend Carolyn Bishop suggested a new punctuation mark, the gravitastrophe. It just happens to be the case that, in times past, in order to make their verse fit the meter, poets would force contractions, syncopes and apocopes (cutting out vowels in the middles or at the ends of words). You might recognize some of these from hymns. This practice is firmly associated with the lofty realm of poetry and thus by itself lends gravitas. By the way, note that all apostrophes are of the 9, not 6, kind; the 6 kind are opening single quotes.

Loving surely

*"F*rankly," I said frankly, "I realize
my problem comes down to your beautiful eyes.
Clearly," I hopefully said, "you can see
the effect that your beauty is having on me."
"Sadly, I do," she replied seriously,
"and, hopefully, this won't come out curiously,
but, unfortunately, I'm not at your disposal;
I've gladly accepted another proposal."
"But, seriously, Shirley," I protested sadly,
"you've seen oh so clearly that I love you madly."
"You do so unfortunately, by sad fate,
for, surely, you see that you're courting too late."
But I suddenly said, "Ere I'm brushed to the curb,
can your paramour handle a sentence adverb?"
And, strangely enough, at this Shirley relented
and, happily, then to my love she consented:
"I'm yours. Suddenly, I see, though you're not early,
I'll happily go with a man who speaks surely."

Here's another area where failure to understand how English works is waved
around as a sign of intellectual superiority. Sentence adverbs - words such as
frankly, seriously, clearly, hopefully, and of course **surely** at the start of a
sentence setting the overall attitude of the sentence rather than modifying the
main verb - have been in use in English at least since the 17th century. The idea
that there's something wrong with them - in particular with just one of them,
hopefully - has only been around since the 20th century, and only really caught
on in the 1960s. Hopefully, this sophomoric foolishness too shall pass.

None of Olive

I had a girl, Olive; she was all of my life,
and all of the time I thought she'd be my wife,
until, out of nowhere, she launched an attack
that all of a sudden threw me all out of whack.

I was being romantic – too much so, it seems –
called her "Olive, my hopes, and Olive, my dreams."
'Twas then that she said the words that still appal:
"That shouldn't be Olive, you know. That's just all."

She said it so quickly, she said it so coolly,
and all of my being she skewered so cruelly.
I ran away then, for it was not to be…
now I search for a girl who will take all of me.

You will find people who will insist – sometimes indignantly – that **all of [this or that]** is flat wrong and should be **all [this or that]** (there are, of course, exceptions to this). I admit it's more economical to leave out the **of**, and it may seem to some a prolix, inelegant innovation to add it, but it is well established in current usage, and it occurs to me that some people value their shibboleths a little too highly and their relations with other people not quite highly enough.

Ellipsis that shall never touch

"*D*ot, Dot, Dot," I asked my belle,
"will you stay and love me well?"
"Darling," she said, "I'll . . . be true;
there's nothing that I'd . . . rather do."

"Dot, Dot, Dot, please let me know,"
I asked her, "if our love will grow."
"My dear, your words are . . . so sublime;
we must together spend . . . sweet time."

"But Dot, Dot, Dot," I said with doubt,
"I sense that you've left something out."
"My words are true, where'er they fall;
not less, not less, I've told you all."

And when she'd spent my funds and left,
'twas then that I, morose, bereft,
saw Dot, Dot, Dot's words reconciled
and knew how I had been beguiled.

Although the words of truth were there,
her ellipsis spoke unfair;
not, less, not, less, had been estranged
and by mean dot, dot, dot exchanged.

The three dots are often used to indicate a pause or a progression of thought, but they can also indicate an omission (as seen in movie ads: "You must ... see this movie!" Hmm... must *not* see it?), and when they do, they're called ellipsis. In the above, the words left out (**not**, **less**, **not**, and **less**) were actually said later. This is not compulsory!

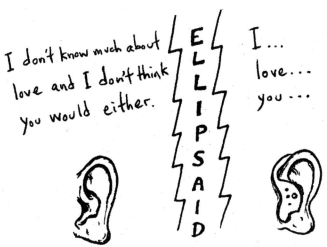

FROM THE MAKERS OF COMMAVISION
AND COLONOSCOPE:

ELLIPSAID HELPS YOU HEAR THE BEST...

She's like all that you know

I know this girl, and she's all that –
she's like, you know, she's got it all,
and she's all "Guys are all like that,
but you're, like, not like that at all."

So I'm like, you know, "What's all that?
So did you dis me? Do you like me?"
And she's "You know it's not, like, that.
You know I know you don't dislike me."

So I'm "Like that's just all I know!
I know you know I know, you know?
So no, it's not a dis, I know."
And she's "I know. I'm just, you know."

But no, you know, it's not like that.
That's just, like, all. It's just, you know?
Cuz that's just her and I'm not that.
I like her, like you know, you know?

But now, you know, it's all "That's all,"
but, like, no, that's not all at all,
cuz she's a girl who has it all,
and, like, I'm just like that, is all.

If you think this tangle of words isn't communicating anything, you've
forgotten what it's like to be a teenager. And if you think that replacing it with
more overt, clear phrasing would mean exactly the same thing, down to the
emotional nuances, then, well, I'm afraid I can't entirely agree with you. Which
is not to say I wouldn't request clarification where possible. But the teenage
years are uncertain and inchoate, and teenage language can sometimes be
thus, too.

An end to selfishness

I asked my love myself last night
just what she thought herself was right
and, if one was oneself in love,
should one's self serve a self above?
She said, "Myself, I think one ought
to move to what one's self is not.
If you yourself have love in store,
then give it to myself for more,
for if you give yourself, you grow;
our selves will join and overflow."
"So if we lose ourselves we gain?
Our selves we give and get? That's plain!"
When we ourselves had this way voiced,
we gave our selves and we rejoiced:
I gave herself my self myself;
she gave myself her self herself;
my self then gave herself her self;
her self, too, gave myself my self.
And then I felt herself in me,
and she myself was there to be,
for to ourselves our selves employ
gave us ourselves a selfless joy!

Reflexive forms – **myself**, **yourself**, etc. – have a long history of being used also as emphatic forms in English. Emphasis is a valuable tool in speech, and vocal emphasis doesn't always accomplish it, so it's good to have this feature, and silly to say there's something wrong with it.

The reflexives have also come to be used as more formal-sounding or less abrupt-sounding versions of the bare pronouns ("You can give it to myself"). Obviously, these forms are not in reality mere reflexives, but you are well within reason and right to wonder if *this* extra bit of verbal clutter is really worth it. Myself, I think perhaps not.

To want, to need, to have

*M*y cousin's friend is kind of lonely.
I owe him. Date her, one night only?
I don't want to, but I have to.

"Put on a suit" is his advice,
"and take her out to someplace nice."
I don't need to, but I have to.

She's pretty, smart – in fact, she's great.
We stay out talking rather late.
I don't need to, but I want to.

At evening's end, to me it's plain:
I'm going to ask her out again.
I don't have to, but I want to.

She says she will. Before we part,
I first must kiss my new sweetheart.
I don't have to, but I need to.

Now I can't live without her near.
I'll end my bachelorhood, I fear!
I don't want to, but I need to.

Although **need** is stronger than **want**, to me, at least, **I don't want** is a stronger rejection than **I don't need** – but I do find that **I don't need** is sometimes used to mean "I need not to have."

Christmas present

*N*ow, Christmas has twelve days, of which the first one is tomorrow,
and I'm giving to my true love all that I can beg or borrow.
She knows that I'm a poet, so I'm giving her my words;
I know that she's allergic, so I'm giving her no birds –
no swans, nor geese, nor turtledoves, nor even partridge one;
I know she's introverted – lords and ladies are no fun.
Loud noises give her headaches. Drummers? Pipers? Please, not now!
And she's getting maids a-milking when she wants to have a cow.
But every year I give her something more than just a rhyme,
and I hope that she says yes to what I'm giving her this time:
on Christmas she is getting all the joy that I can bring,
for tomorrow I am giving her not five, but one gold ring.
She knows I don't have money, but she knows she has my love;
with her I know I'm gifted by an angel from above.
So tomorrow I am proving what tonight I'm here to tell:
there's nothing like the present to begin the future well.

In English, we don't have a single-word inflection for the future tense. We
have auxiliaries - notably **will** - but we also use the present tense to speak of
the future (in fact, those auxiliaries were also originally verbs conjugated in
the present tense). We also use it for durable states (**she knows I don't have
money**) and habitual acts (**every year I give her**). This poem talks a lot about
the future, but have a look: every verb in it is conjugated in the present.

PG-rated (just a little naughty)

&!

*T*he ampersand. That little snake.
You let it in, your heart will break.
Love & marriage, Mom & Pop,
hearth & home… I have to stop.
I'm lost & lonely, tired & sad,
& this ill squiggle makes me mad,
& yet some people find it h&y
to pop it here & there like c&y.
I once knew a girl, Am&a,
who wrote me little memor&a:
"Let's meet & eat & have some fun";
"I'm good & ready, you're the one";
"You & I are hand & glove –
let's bump & grind & make some love."
She was r&y, I confess,
but l&ed me in some distress
when, after weeks of fun & joy,
she p&ered to another boy,
some guy called &y, for a lark –
some manh&ling in car in dark.
Her belly sometime thence exp&ed;
little tests were thus comm&ed;
they said &y was the sire…
so was gone my heart's desire.
&y did the noble thing:
he h&ed her a diamond ring.
Now they're mom & dad & child,
& ampers&s just make me wild.
I wish that they would all be b&,
but they persist in my own h&.
I can't stop, to my regret;
I hold a c&le for her yet.

Some people use the ampersand just too darn much.

By the way, it comes from a stylized form of the Latin word for and, **et**. Some type faces make this more apparent: picture a Greek-style (or cursive capital) E and a small t joined together. Now close the top of the E into a loop, tilt the t, and stylize it a little more.

A romantic conversion

*W*hile hoofing down the street one day, I eyed a girl so fair
and glimpsed her smiling back at me and toying with her hair.

By nature she was gifted with a look that none could match,
but 'twas her way of speeching that was what you'd want to catch –

for when I wished her happy day, and hoped I wasn't rude,
she giggled, "You look good to me. Let's walk, and then let's food."

Therefore we strolled and chatted some, and, spotting a café,
seated ourselves to sip some tea and try some verbal play.

"Now, I'm a normal girl," she mouthed, "but habit one perversion:
I hope you will not grudge me if I voice that it's conversion."

Conversion! Ah, she thrilled me when the word by her was tabled.
I twigged I faced the verbing girl, whose lingual skills were fabled.

She purred, "There's one thing I must clear: although I like to verb,
I do not prejudice so much; my tongue I will not curb

if native verb would kiss my lips, if it has yet been nouned;
I also need auxiliaries and 'be' to talk around."

I spouted then to her my case, that I and she did pair;
she grinned, and winked, and stroked my face, and sighed that it was fair.

But if I hoped to stay, she whispered, I did face one choice:
the only deeds that we could act were ones that we could voice.

"I will not make a pure move conversion's never touched."
I nodded that I did assent, and so our hands we clutched.

Then from our tea we legged it back to nest at her retreat
and huddled there and couched ourselves and planned a future sweet.

Now we may shout but rarely fight; we rhyme, we dance, we trust,
and now and then we will conversion new verbs as we must –

but all the verbs conversion's granted us set rare the need
for stunts to sustenance our body English sweet indeed.

Verbing is another thing that sets some people off. You will find people who will swear it's a sign of laxity and degradation in the language. Actually, conversion – of nouns to verbs, of verbs to nouns, of nouns to adjectives, of adjectives to adverbs, etc. – is one of the most important and time-honoured ways of adding words to English and of keeping communication clear and efficient. Every single verb in the above poem (except for versions of **be** and auxiliaries such as **do** and **will**) either was created by conversion ("verbing") from a noun or has a noun version in the language that has been produced by conversion, in every case without addition of a suffix. Obviously some of the verbs above are newly converted. But every conversion was new at some time!

And who shall I say is colon?

The colon: like two beady eyes,
an adder lurking in disguise –
or like the holes left in your skin
when adder's added venom in.

When eyes peek out from verbal woods,
in what comes next you'll get the goods –
but always when the adder adds,
you know you'll get less goods than bads.

"Dear applicant:" the letter starts;
you'll know the message really smarts.
"Dear occupant:" means "hit the street";
"To whom it may concern:" defeat.

"Total owing:" says the bill,
and then it closes for the kill.
"FYI:" adds work to do;
"To wit:" means "witless – that means you."

The snake that lets you know you're gone
will bite you when you read "Dear John:"
– but adder-eyes that most insults
may be the one on "Test results:"

And even when you think there's hope,
when snake-bite comes, forget it. Nope.
"Here are the winners:" reads the host...
Go get a drink. You know you're toast.

For colon-clenching explanation,
there is no known inoculation.
The text it adds subtracts from you.
Face it: there's nothing you can do.

I've long thought of the colon as like a pair of expectant eyes. What is on one
side depends in some way on what is on the other - often, as above, it's an
introduction; at other times, the text after is the punch line to a longer bit of text
before.

Dim innuendos

A sweet musician in a bar said, "Boy, I think you're #."
I said, "Girl, you're a ♮, but I don't want to harp."
She said, "Well, here's the key so you can get into my ♭."
The rest of it I can't repeat, so I'll conclude at that.

Sharp, natural, flat. I didn't think it would be wise to try to include a repeat typographically – it doesn't really work without the rest of the bar lines.

Don't tell me no lies

I met a little lady from way down south
and I thought she was kinda sweet.
She had a tasty tongue in a cowgirl mouth
that said things you'd wanna repeat.

"I don't never go for that city stuff –
I like my drinks and men smooth and hard."
And I said, "Won't you leave me when you've had enough?"
And she said, handing back my credit card,

"I don't want none of your money, sweet,
I don't care for no one but you.
I don't know nothin' 'bout how to cheat –
that ain't nothin' I'd wanna do."

We had a little drink and we had a little dance
and we painted lots of red on the town,
and pretty soon we had ourselves a fine romance
and I took her out shopping for a gown.

Oh, I bought her a ring, and I bought her a home,
and I got her set up nice and neat.
But sometimes I'd worry she would use me and roam,
and whenever I did, she'd repeat,

"I don't want none of your money, sweet,
I don't care for no one but you.
I don't know nothin' 'bout how to cheat –
that ain't nothin' I'd wanna do."

So now why am I sittin' with my head hangin' low
with nothin' left, not even pride,
wonderin' where my sweetheart and my money did go
and how I got took for a ride?

My gal was a master of verbal predation,
a lawyer who took her reward –
she tripped up my ears with double negation
that I thought was negative concord:

"I don't want none of your money, sweet,
I don't care for no one but you.
I don't know nothin' 'bout how to cheat –
that ain't nothin' I'd wanna do."

The double negative is one thing the prescriptivists won on. English had negative concord for a long time - if you negate one part of a phrase, you negate them all for consistency, just as in some languages you make the adjective feminine if the noun is, for instance. Romance languages still use negative concord. But by the 19th century it was pretty much vanquished in English by appeal to "logic" (rather than appeal to Latin, which actually uses negative concord). And yet in many "nonstandard" versions of English it's still used - and understood. After all, language doesn't actually work like math. But the "standard" rules - put in place by the legal class, in fact - are what prevail in law.

Oh, and all those **-in'** endings? That's another thing prescriptivists won on. By the 18th century, the **-ing** suffix had come to be pronounced as "-in" by everyone (because the tongue is drawn forward by the vowel); rhymes by English poets of the time don't work with the "ing" version. But the spelling hadn't changed, and so it was insisted by those who taught the stuff that the ending should be pronounced as written. Nonetheless, while the formal standard has changed, the old way hasn't been eradicated. By the way, saying "-in" isn't actually dropping the **g**; there is no **g** to drop (**ng** is just how we write the sound - do you heard a "g" in there? only in words like **finger**). It's just fronting the consonant - from the velum (at the back of the mouth) to the alveolar ridge (near the front).

getting naked

i met a woman young and fair
who liked her skin to feel the air
now im not wedded to convention
but i felt some apprehension
when i got to know her better
and she sent me this short letter
it is time that i should tell
i keep my text au naturel
i know that this will sound uncouth
but i believe in naked truth
in every place and situation
shed the chains of punctuation
doff the clothes of upper case
and stand revealed on white space
now i dont mind it being nude
but naked text at first seemed crude
however now its plain to see
that form and sense are both more free
and so we read our morning papers
sprawled in bed we serve up capers
in the kitchen we grow flowers
in the garden we take showers
in the bathroom we go hiking
on the mountains its our liking
to go swimming every day
in the pond in a cafe
sip a coffee or just run
on the trail our life is fun
my only cause for consternation
is some miscommunication
if my lover should insist
on writing on the shopping list
get some mustard greens and tea
do i buy two things or three

and now i have this little note
that concerns me and i quote
darling i think love is great
with others i would hesitate
to give my all to none but you
i feel open can you too
as i read it twice im guessing
if shes offering her blessing
to monogamous relation
or some other situation
its one thing when going shopping
now im faced with chamber hopping
in this textual revolution
can i find a real solution

Quite something, isn't it, how much you can understand without any
punctuation or capitalization. And how much you can't.

I, woe is me...

I met this very nice guy,
but one thing could just make me die:
his pet phrase, "Between you and I."

This usage made me wince,
but, with harsh words, I mince,
so I just tried dropping hints.

"My friend has asked us to tea,
and wonders how many there'll be.
Shall I say to expect you and *me*?"

"Yes, expect you and I," he replied.
I almost could have cried;
I stifled a shudder and sighed.

"My friends seem to have conspired.
Do you think it would be desired
to trust he and she?" I inquired.

His expression was slightly pained.
"I don't know just what would be gained...
between you and I," he explained.

And so it went on in this way,
from day to maddening day,
no matter what I'd say:

"Give it to he and her,"
"You and me would prefer,"
"To I it would occur..."

You really would expect
he'd sort out what's correct,
but he kept the defect.

It came that, eventually,
I said, "It is easy to see
something's come between you and me."

He said, "Indeed, I've waited
for change while we have dated,
but you sound... uneducated."

At that, I dropped my preference
for passiveness and deference,
went home, and got a reference,

and, just for exercise,
and to repay surprise,
whacked him between the I's.

"Between you and I" is an example of a common hypercorrection – many of us, when children, were told, after we said something like "Mike and me are going to the store," that it was "Mike and I," but somehow never quite picked up that you only use **I** in a combination when it's the subject of a sentence – in other words, just where you would use **I** by itself. So if you say "Give it to me" rather than "Give it to I" (and I expect you do, unless you speak one of several West Indian dialects), you should say "Give it to Mike and me" – and also "between you and me" (just as you would say "between him and her" rather than "between he and she"). It's fascinating, though, isn't it, how we don't do this automatically – it seems that multiple subjects aren't handled in the brain in the same way as individual ones are.

A heroic tale

I read an historical story
in a book I bought last year
of an hideous, horrible monster
that brought an town much fear.

This beast, with fangs and claws,
in an hidden hovel waited,
and a passer-by who'd pause
would be disarticulated:

he'd become an passer-by,
and in an horrible state
(who would not rather die
than face such an horrid fate?).

And since this hideous fiend
lay right by the borough's border,
soon all townsmen were demeaned
with their articles out of order.

When a hero from foreign place
heard of this ogre's game,
he called it a disgrace
and in a hurry came.

But when he drew an sword,
he saw he'd been affected;
by the fiend he had been gored
in an moment undetected.

He knew that he must think
and composure gain again,
for he was on the brink
of meeting an horrible n.

Just then, a maiden came
and said, "May I disturb?
You might just win this game
if you'll but use an herb."

"An herb!" He thought. "A flower!
Why, that seems just absurd!"
But then he saw the power
that came from that small word:

for when a herb he used
in place of swinging blade,
the beast became confused
and quickly was unmade –

for it could do no harm
where it could do no wrong,
and so a maiden's charm
bid an ugly beast so long.

"Who are you," the hero cried,
"to be with words so prudent?"
"Kind sir," the lass replied,
"I'm just an articling student."

And in a historic moment,
the hero beat sword to plow
and pledged to follow the maiden
(well, she's not a maiden now).

One of English's inflexibly consistent rules is the one governing the indefinite article: use **a** when the next word starts with a consonant sound and **an** when the next word starts with a vowel sound. So **a university** but **an hour**. We will notice that **h**, when pronounced – as in **hotel** and **historical** – is undoubtedly a consonant in English. We say **a hallucination**, for instance. With **herb**, you choose **a** or **an** according to your pronunciation.

There was, however, a time when the French influence had English speakers dropping that initial **h** sound, and so words that began with **h** got **an** before them. However, in most dialects, the **h** is back in place in most of these words. But printed matter is resistant to change, because you can still see the older versions. It took longer for the **an** to disappear before **h**-words in print; a hundred years ago – or should I say an hundred years ago – quite a few words starting with an **h** sound still got **an**. By the end of the 20th century, only one still occasionally got the **an**: **historic** (or **historical**), perhaps because it's used in more formal and pompous occasions, and people tend to assume that a weird exception they see in older texts must be more formally correct. Well, it's not. It's a mumpsimus – a mistaken idea clung to stubbornly. Some people will even say that you drop the **h** – but only in **historic** and **historical**, of course – after **an**. In reality, the form of the word without the article always determines the article, not the other way. English has exceptions to its rules, of course, but this isn't one, and it has no sensible reason to be considered one; its only value is as a shibboleth.

¶

*T*he pilcrow is a funny thing:
in place of beak, it has a bump;
a pair of lines in place of wing;
no sign of feathers, feet, or rump.

It has a rather narrow niche,
the which it fills with neat precision,
slipping in where there's a wish
to break a flow or cause division.

And while a normal crow will fly
and seize its food with beak or claws,
the pilcrow likes to linger by
and do its work by means of pause.

In every place you need a tear,
in every place you need a laugh,
step back: the pilcrow will appear
to start another paragraph.

"Is this your car? You have it made."
Pilcrow. "It's cheap – you'd never guess it.
Not really – I just haven't paid."
Pilcrow. "I'm here to repossess it."

"You have the check, but will you mate?"
Pilcrow. "Let's recommence the game.
I'll see you at the garden gate."
Pilcrow. Alas, he never came.

"That girl you saw? She's just my cousin."
Pilcrow. "One more? I never knew."
Pilcrow. "Oh, yes, I've had a dozen."
Pilcrow. "Take back your ring. We're through."

If life is humorous or hollow,
you need to crow, or get last word,
or life's a bitter pill, don't swallow;
you'll find the pilcrow is your bird.

The pilcrow – ¶ – is the symbol (when needed) for a paragraph break.

Everyone's a diacritic

I thought Božena worth a whirl,
but she was just a háček girl.
Käthe bored me right to pieces –
she had verbal dieresis.
Siân was not inclined to sex;
she was just too circumflex.
Françoise gave more than my fill –
she just couldn't sit cedille.
Åsa went for everything,
but kept on pushing for a ring.
Begoña wasn't so sublime
to stay with tilde end of time.
I knew Michèle was not the one…
a bit too grave to be much fun.
Ah, but Renée was heaven sent:
vivacious, with acute accent!

Admittedly, hat check girls aren't all that common anymore. Some of these diacritical marks have other names as well – a háček is also called a caron, for instance, a ring is also called a kroužek, and a dieresis is perhaps better known as an umlaut (after the phonological transformation it marks in German).

Unrequoted love

I'm getting letters from my dear,
but I'm not sure that she's sincere.
I see the way she ends her notes:
the phrase *"I love you"* is in quotes.
I really don't know what to do,
for if she's quoting, quoting who?

Although I know it seems absurd,
her every gift is but a word:
I send you "hugs", I send you "kisses" –
That's it? Some kind of present this is!
She writes, *I "miss" you,* and I see
the missing is mere irony!

Well, I think I know what to do:
I'm writing her, *I "miss" you too.*
My "love" is such, if you were here,
you'd get "a diamond ring", my dear.
My "life" shall be at your disposal –
I wait for "yes" to my "proposal".

She sends mere quotes? I send her same!
She'll know that two can play this game!

Quotation marks are not suitable for conveying emphasis. They're made to
indicate that the material within them is quoted, either from a real person or
from some postulated "they" (as in "They say that..."). They thus distance the
speaker from the contents and may as such also be used to convey irony or to
make the subject the words themselves rather than what they convey.

May is for lovers

I met a girl called Dorothy
who seemed a bit reserved to me.
I asked her, "Can I call you Dot?"
She said, "You can, but you may not."

But she had charm with her froidure,
and looks – I thought I'd try a cure:
"Well, can I say you're kind of hot?"
"You can," she said, "but you may not."

I thought I might have spied a wink,
and so I offered her a drink.
"Then can I buy you beer? A shot?"
"You can, oh, yes. But you may not."

Every offer she resisted,
but I liked her; I persisted:
"Can I ask you out? I ought!"
"You can," she smiled, "but you may not."

At last I got her on a date,
and, mister, I could hardly wait.
"Now, can I make this work?" I thought.
I heard, "You can, but you may not!"

I drove her to a scenic view
with hopes for all the things we'd do,
but when we reached the smooching spot,
she said "You can, but you may not."

But then, in that remote location,
the angel of equivocation
told me just what I should say:
"I may not; then again, I may!"

She blushed; she smiled; she cocked her head;
"You may? Well, then, you must," she said.
"I must? I will, if you so bid,"
I said. And so, at that, we did.

Some people insist that **can** refers to ability and **may** to permission – thus
the teacher asked by a student "Can I go to the washroom?" might say "You
can, but you may not," meaning "You have the ability but not the permission."
However, this distinction is not maintained by too many people other than
pedants. Even Tennyson didn't stick to it, and he's a revered English author. But
one thing that is true (and you can use this to your advantage) is that **may** can
also refer to possibility – if you say something may happen, you might just be
saying that there's the chance of its happening, not that it has the permission to
happen. And even pedants have to acknowledge this sense.

James Harbeck

Your asterisk

You have a little trouble that pops your little bubble?
Your dark sword of romance is sleeping in your pants?
Take our pill when you frisk – we'll fix you.*

You're stuck at your computer and feeling kind of neuter?
You want to add some spice? Our software is quite nice.
It's all here on this disk – install it.*

A horse has you impressed? You're wanting to invest
if you could get a chance? We'll lend you an advance!
Our service will be brisk – and friendly.*

Your third trip down the aisle, you've found one who's worthwhile?
And just to firm it up, she gives you a pre-nup?
Don't fear; you'll share the risk – forever.*

You may not have a hunch there's never a free lunch,
but lawyers have their laws and kittens have their clause.
You leap in blind? Tsk, tsk... Well, it's your *.

---

* Your results may vary. For best results, say "asterisk" wherever you see the
mark above...

Were or was it so

*W*ere subjunctives not to be,
it would be a tragedy:
I would spend my life not knowing
if love *was* – or *were* – still glowing.
Was or *were* I still your lover…
was it done? could I discover?
Was I lying there beside you?
Were I there, no harm betide you!
It were sweetest song to me
to know it *was*, not *were*, to be.
If I were your paramour,
would our love come from before?
If I *was* your lover, o,
that is something I should know.
If I were imagining things –
Wait! That phrase means truth still rings!
If I was deluded, then
would I were so dazed again!
Subjunctive, be the mood that sets
dreams apart from past regrets.

English has different moods for its verbs – the normal one is the indicative; if
you give an order, it's the imperative (**be the mood**); if you speak of something
that is known not to be currently the case, it's the subjunctive. Not everyone
uses special verb forms for the subjunctive anymore, but they do allow
distinctions for those who use them. **If I were** presupposes that I am not
and postulates the possibility in the present ("If I were a rich man"); **if I was**
examines a question of a past state in reality ("If I was unintentionally rude, I
apologize"). **It were** is an archaic form now; it means "it would be."

The one

*I'*m dating a girl who likes moderation
but sometimes praises without reservation.
She has a cute way to show you your place:
she starts off partway, then slips you the ace.

I cooked her some dinner on our first date.
"That's one of the best meal I ever ate!"
She said that. One best! A class of one!
Such flattery! And we'd just begun.

We went to a movie – the choice was clear:
"It's one of the best film of the year,"
she said. "On that, the critics agree."
(They'd all gone for this one? That's news to me!)

As we walked back, the weather was just sublime:
"It's one of the nicest night in quite a time."
It was clear in all that she had to say
that she wanted to take things all the way.

At evening's end, she gave me my throne:
"one of the best lover I've ever known."
"Lover," not "lovers" – now, how do you do:
on the list of the best, there's no number two!

It looks like the matter is when, not whether,
we'll be vowing to share the future together.
Her level of commitment is plain to see:
"You're one of the only guy for me."

This one is similar to the false concord issue above, and it's a very common thing to see. The analytically "correct" way to put something like this – and the way that seems more natural to at least some of us – is to say, for instance, **one of the best lovers**. That is, there's a set of people who are the best lovers, and the person in question is one of them. And, indeed, even people who would say or write **one of the best lover** would, I think, write **one of them** rather than **one of him** for short. But because the subject of the sentence is singular, and we have **one** as well, there's a certain magnetism of singularity, shall we say. The speaker stays focused on the one person and uses **one of the best** as though it were **a one-of-the-best** or **a top-quality** to modify **lover**. Frankly, I'd still rather use the plural there – it just makes more sense to me.

Not that many of us are necessarily all that used to hearing the phrase in the first place.

Not enough

She asked for love; she gave me much;
I hardly gave her any such.
She wanted more; I gave her less –
that wasn't very nice, I guess.
And kisses? Oh, she gave me many,
although I hardly gave her any.
She wanted more; I gave her fewer –
I hankered after someone newer.
My love was after all of me,
but it was not at all to be,
and after all our joy and fun,
I had her all and gave her none.
At all the times I had her yet,
I still was after all I'd get,
but when she got no love or kisses,
she said, "Some kind of romance this is.
I'll find some love with someone good
who'll give some kisses when he should."
And when she'd heard another's call,
I found I loved her after all.

I'm not really making a point here. I'm just playing with quantity words for countables (**many**) and mass objects (**much**) and then going nuts with **all** and **after all**.

More downs than ups

To live it up on Saturday I went out on the town
and did some things I find I'm having trouble living down.
I saw a girl and tried to pick her up – without success;
in fact, I'd have to say the lady picked me down, I guess.
I tried a line to butter her up, but what I thought was wit
came out sounding rather wrong and buttered her down a bit.
I tried to smarten up and think up how I could reverse,
but smartened down and thought down; every word just made it worse.
She wanted me to give up and wrap up, but I would not;
I gave down and wrapped down, and in the end my tongue was caught.
Every move I made just fixed things down a little more,
and every minute she was perked down farther than before.
At length, her drink was empty, and I thought I saw a chance;
I filled it up – but then I filled it down, onto her pants.
She cheered down quite completely and she walked away from me,
and I was left as pent down as a healthy guy can be.
The moral of this story, if there's one that may be said,
is know when to shut up, or you'll just get shut down instead.

What's up with all that? I'm not down with it!

47

James Harbeck

She cast a spelling on me

Now, I'm a Yank, but I have class:
I'm going with a British lass,
and, just to keep our entente warm,
I've changed my spellings to her norm.

It's quite the storey, our romance;
to start, it hardly had a chance.
I'll tell you how we came to meet
at a metre by the street.

I parked my car and walked about,
saw her, and went to cheque her out.
Her uniform plainly displayed
her office as a metre maid.

She stood by cars... she stood by *mine*...
she stood there draughting me a fine!
I was gobsmacked, couldn't hack it,
struck too dumb to raise a racquet.

Then she left. I had to catch her!
I made a call to her despatcher.
He said he'd send her back my way.
I tried to practice what I'd say.

She came; I felt light as a feather.
I said, "It's quite the barmy weather!"
But she was cool, this pommy lass,
and I felt rather like an arse.

I knew she saw that I was smitten;
alas, the ticket still was written.
I was wrong – I could not refute her,
could not reprogramme her computer.

I made small talk to keep her by
and fan the embers in her eye.
I feared that she might tyre, yet
I'd clearly fallen in her nett.

At last she said she'd come with me
that evening for a cup of tea.
The reason that she chose to go?
My way with words impressed her so!

This dude has managed to press a bunch of British spellings (some of which are common in Canada but are not used in the US) into incorrect service. **Storey** means a level of a building, not a tale (story). **Metre** is a unit of measurement, not something that measures (meter). **Cheque** is a bank draft, not an inspection or to inspect (check). **Draught** is a noun, as in wind or beer, not a verb meaning to draw up (draft). **Racquet** is what you play various sports with, not a loud noise (racket). **Despatch** is speed, not sending people or things forth (dispatch). **Practice** is a noun; the verb is practise. **Barmy** means crazy, not warm (balmy). An **arse** is one's hindquarters, not a donkey or a fool (ass). **Reprogramme** is actually OK, as **programme** is the British spelling for program in whatever sense – but the Brits would more likely stick a hyphen in, re-programme. **Tyre** is the thing a car drives on, not the verb meaning to fatigue (tire). **Nett** means total after deductions, not a meshwork (net).

The restrictive which

*T*here is a certain house which sits upon a shady street
and in it lives a person which you may not want to meet.

She has a cloak and hat which she is never seen without
and owns a darkling cat which likes to yowl and prowl about.

And there is one key thing which makes this witch a cause of fear:
she has a special magic which she does to those who near.

Whatever thing she catches which is single of its kind,
she makes it simply that which is like others you may find.

This is an operation which she does with neat precision
by writing sentences which are subjected to excision

of one small curly mark which serves to separate the noun
from modifying phrase which newly serves to tie it down.

No longer have you just one job, which pays you well, to work;
your job which pays you well shares time with other jobs which shirk.

You had a dent, which is not big, alone upon your car;
now by the dent which is not big sit other dents that are.

Your marriage, which is happy, soon will find it's not alone –
your marriage which is happy won't be when the rest are known.

Your ring, which says Eileen, will lead Eileen to know your games:
your ring which says Eileen shares space with rings with other names.

It's bad enough to have one bad divorce, which is near done;
the bad divorce which is near done awaits another one,

and though one lawyer's bill, which could be worse, is not a lot,
the bill which could be worse is stacked with others which could not.

And all this loss which is not fair comes not from peeve or itch;
it comes from lack of caution with that bad restrictive witch.

A nonrestrictive clause is one that simply describes the thing just mentioned
without further limiting it – if you have one house, and it's big, then it's
your house, which is big. A restrictive clause further specifies the thing just
mentioned – if you say **your house which is big**, you're specifying which
house you're talking about (the big one), and that implies that you also have
at least one house which is not big. Now, it's more common in North America
to use **that** rather than **which** for restrictive clauses (**your house that is big**),
but **which** is normal in England and elsewhere and many people use it in
North America. The thing that makes the difference between the two kinds of
clause (in print) is the comma: with a comma, it's nonrestrictive; without, it's
restrictive, which (perhaps confusingly) means that there is more than one of
the thing described.

Unromantic interlude (not about love etc.)

Getting around efficiently

*O*h, all the places we have gone –
we've seen Forts Myers and St. John;
Green and Thunder Bays were nice,
and Frobisher, though full of ice;
Long and Virginia Beaches – spiffy;
Grand and Cedar Rapids – iffy;
I still recall how we did things
in Hot and Colorado Springs
and Sans Diego and Jose –
oh, yes, and don't forget ta Fe;
Saints Petersburg and Paul were green,
Dart and Fal mouths were marine;
Ott and Osh awas were cool;
Grands Forks and Rapids, rather cruel;
Cals gary and ifornia, great;
Monts pelier and réal – don't wait;
Winds dsor and nipeg, give a miss;
Den and Vancou vers, skiers' bliss;
Columbs us and ia, just fair;
Phoeni and Bron xes – don't go there;
Moose Jaw and Factory – no way;
Jun and Gatin eaux – OK;
Toes peka, ledo, ronto – yeah;
Men chester and itoba – nah.
Oh, yes, we've had the time that was
in Canad and Americ as!

When you're referring to a couple of geographical features, such as the Bow River and the Elbow River, you can join them together and say the **Bow and Elbow rivers**, because **river** can be treated as a descriptive term in this case. If you're talking about Green Bay and North Bay, you can say **Green and North bays** if you're talking about the bays, but it might be misleading to use that when you're talking about the cities. Some people like to extend this practice to city names, as in **Forts Meyers and St. John**, but that can get a little dodgy.

A horror movie/scary story

A girl/young woman/female juvenile
was found late one evening/at night
in a bad/sorry state in her domicile,
huddled up/wide-eyed/quaking with fright.

The sliding door/window had gone off its track,
forced away by the housebreaker/crasher,
and the lawmen arriving were taken aback:
"Call the captain in! We've got a slasher!"

The young victim/witness explained with sobs/tears
that her life was so easy before,
but now she'd faced evil/the sum of her fears,
nothing seemed sure anymore.

How could she lounge in the living room/den
and read books/play X-Box/watch TV,
or feel safe on the patio/verandah again
when she wouldn't know just where she'd be?

Her felines/cats Fluffy and Patches had been
made companion animals/pets
and would probably have to be treated/seen
by animal doctors/vets.

The constable asked where her parents were.
She sobbed/wailed, "Upstairs/second floor.
You'll find my adults/parents/guardians there
hiding/locked in/concealed by a door."

Although the group/family passed the ordeal
without any bruise/wound/contusion,
the constable knew/had a hunch/went by feel
they were out of sorts/left in confusion.

And just then did the copper/fuzz twig/realize
that the slasher was still there/around,
and he rallied his men/he called on the guys
to hunt/look/seek till he was caught/found.

But the slasher escaped while the men were in doubt,
and no one knows where he could be...
So we'd better be vigilant/keep an eye out.
Oh no! He's slashed/gotten to me!

Although the slash is commonly used to indicate alternatives (**read books/
play X-Box/watch TV**), combinations (**victim/witness**), or alternative terms
for the same thing (**felines/cats**), I would recommend against trying the above
at home.

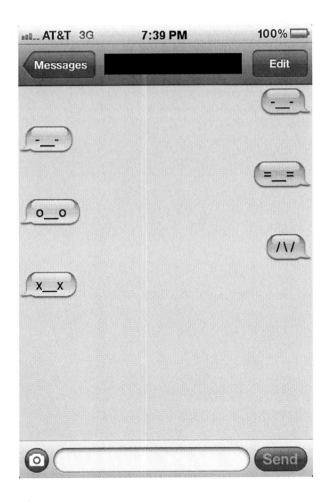

A textual treatment

I've found it's rather dry of late –
my "little marks" have all gone straight.
Apostrophes, quotation marks,
they're limp, as if they've lost their sparks.
I'm saying to myself, "Well, surely,
there's a way to make them curly."
And so I've found this little firm
that's going to give my text a perm.

OK, it's done. Is it impressive?
It might be just a touch excessive.
My "little marks" are really swell,
but other things have curled as well ~
my v is like a candy dish,
my l like steam, my dash a swish ~
but if one thing takes me aback, it's
what's become of {these} my brackets!

True, in italics a dash doesn't become a tilde and square brackets don't become curly brackets. So?

But why not?

$\mathcal{A}$nd can it be that I should gain
and "and" or "but" without compunction?
Or should I start my words in vain
if they're begun with a conjunction?

For I am told that such a choice
displays a lack of erudition.
But flow and tone can lose their voice
if words are forced out of position.

Nor can proscribers show just why
this thought-flow-damming rule should be.
Yet they persist. But I say fie!
And I shall flout them merrily.

Here's something that many people "know" is wrong. But it's not wrong at all.
Sentences have been started with conjunctions in English for centuries, and by
many of the most respected English authors. The insistence that this produces
a sentence fragment is merely a product of mental inflexibility: someone has
decided that a sentence must be a certain way, and if sentences occur any
other way, they're not sentences. It's rather like a birdwatcher saying "Ostriches
aren't birds. They don't fly. Obviously they can't be birds!"

Pause for a moment and think of the people you know who freely start
sentences with conjunctions when it's useful for the flow. Then think of the
people you know who would berate you for doing so. Which set of people do
you like better? Which set of people do you respect more? And which set are
truly able to communicate more effectively? Now, given that starting sentences
with conjunctions is a well-established practice even among some of the most
liked and respected English authors, whose version of the language do you
really want to adhere to?

The life of a hyphen

*H*ow hard to be a hyphen
and have to spend your life in
a word gap so slim-spaced
you couldn't stick a knife in,

to be miscalled a dash
(though you lack the panache) –
or else to be replaced,
here/there bumped by a slash.

And what must truly hurt
is how few are alert
to rules that determine
just where they should insert

your quick-tossed little stay,
so quick tossed by the way
by know-naught scribbling vermin
who know naught good to say.

Who knows if you can face
elision by a space
word joining just by breath,
devoid of inky lace,

and Heaven only knows your
chances of composure
faced with certain death
in some wordjamming closure.

The mark to the right of 0 on your keyboard, -, though it is often called a dash, is in fact a hyphen. (See the next poem for dashes.) Among other things (such as indicating that a word has broken at a line end), it is often used to join words that have been made into compounds, either established ones (such as **clip-on**) or ones that are made on the spot as compound modifiers (such as **slim-spaced** and **know-naught**). Many people don't bother with the hyphen and just let the two words stand side by side (which would make, for example, "quick tossed little stay" and "know naught scribbling vermin"), but this can produce ambiguities. On the other hand, sometimes the words are just stuck together, which is also what German does. Hyphens are more often killed in the word compactor when they join a prefix and a word, as in **e-mail**, which is now very commonly **email**.

A thorn in my heart

I write in longing for the thorn,
that runic glyph indicative
of interdental fricative
that from our writing has been torn.

The sound it marks is native bred,
but somewhere in the Middle Age
some French type knocked it off the page
and now we use T H instead.

And where they wished to let it be,
what really makes me want to die
is, lacking thorn, they just used Y
so "the" could be misread as "ye"!

Now "ye" survives as archaism
on signs like "Ye Olde Candy Shoppe,"
reanalyzed – oh, stop, please stop!
It's giving me an aneurysm!

And this is a most bitter pill
because, if we should want to use it,
computers now will let use choose it –
it seems Icelandic has it still.

O, let us now bring back the thorn
and, while we're at it, eth and ash –
our typeset has *them* in its stash.
Our script without is left forlorn!

The thorn, which originally was for the voiceless wound at the end of "with" but later in English came also to stand for the voiced equivalent at the start of "the," looks like this: Þ and þ. It's used only for the voiceless sound in Icelandic. The eth, which is for the voiced sound (as in "the") in Old English and Icelandic, though it gradually became interchangeable with thorn before being tossed out of English, looks like this: Ð and ð. Ash (or æsc) stood for the vowel sound in "at," though in modern Icelandic it sounds like English "eye"; it's Æ and æ.

All right? Alright! I'll write.

*W*elcome to play school. You'll find that it's fun.
I'll tell you, kid, you've got it alright here.

After cookies and juice, your playtime's begun.
So let's play house – you've got a doll right here.

Now, I'll play the mom and you'll play the son.
So here's your lunch. You've got it all, right here.

Then we'll send you to school to start grade one.
These are your books. You've got it all, right? Here.

Now I'll play the teacher, Sister Rosie, a nun.
This is the class. You've got it alright? Here,

do this small quiz – keep on till you're done.
This is your pen. You've got it all. Write here.

Wow, through just like that? You're pretty quick, hon.
And very smart, too – you've got it all right here.

Now let's play gym. Can you roll, jump and run?
Wow! You have skill – you've got it, alright. Here,

time for report cards. You've sure learned a ton.
Now where's the pen? You've got it. I'll write here.

My teacher's remarks: You're second to none!
What a fun day. You've got it alright here.

You have, undoubtedly, encountered at some time the vehement insistence that **alright** is not a word, merely a mark of illiteracy and intellectual inferiority. And yet no one inveighs so against **already** or **almost**. True, **alright** doesn't have quite the pedigree those others have – the evidence is that its modern form was created by analogy a bit over a century ago, and that **all right** is the original form – but there are many newer words that are well accepted. And why shouldn't we be able to make a distinction between "entirely correct" and "OK"?

Some of the other phrases (e.g., **you've got a doll right here**) don't sound the same for people in many parts of the world – the neutralization of **t** and **d** in some contexts by conversion to a tap is particular mainly to North American dialects. But **write** and **right** sound the same everywhere – you might think the **w**, but you round your lips no more or less in **write** than in **right**.

The grapes of disagreement

$\mathcal{T}$he grapes in the orchard is ripe and ready,
the orchard of the grapes are quite well tended,
the scent of the grapes are fresh and heady,
yet problems will soon be apprehended.

The glasses of juice is ready to serve,
the juice in the glasses are nice and sweet,
yet the server of the glasses surely deserve
some glasses and juice that's a better treat.

The vines in the spring was tended neatly
by a tender of the grapes that knew their craft,
but the grafter was busy whispering sweetly
to his mistress, and not watching, when he did the graft.

The drinkers of the juice raises glasses to quaff
in a sweet anticipation of a sweet reward,
but the taste in the mouth will always be off
when the grapes to make the juice is false concord.

Concord, grammatically, is another word for agreement, such as between noun and verb – **the grapes are ready** rather than **the grapes is ready**, for instance. False concord is when the verb agrees with the wrong noun. You'll actually see this fairly often – when there's a complex construction, sometimes the actual noun that's the subject of the sentence will be too far from the verb and the author will conjugate for a closer noun (another noun in a prepositional phrase, such as **of the grapes**). Funny to think that we can construct sentences complex enough that by the time we have them all spoken or written out we've lost track of some of the grammatical relationships.

Cat-ese on the keys

I have a cat. It's very clever.
It doesn't speak too well, however.
But does that stop a smart feline
from sending messages? Not mine!

If Cleo has some thing to say,
she's found a quite efficient way:
my keyboard is the medium –
she types with paws and, sometimes, bum.

OK, it's not in English, yes,
but it's a language nonetheless.
I've studied what comes through the keys
and now I'm fluent in cat-ese.

If she should, just by force of paw,
type .l, juh vffc swa
it's just a note while passing through
she's left to tell me "I love you."

If with her bum and body weight
she types mcvnldkfjghouiyt578
I know that she's not being rude;
she's simply saying "Give me food."

And if, with full-length force of fur,
she makes /,lll-p09o0zs43dw5.0ok9in9ngv7y7c65d4er
then that means, as you may have guessed,
she's telling me "Time for a rest."

I'd write a book, but I expect
that each cat has a dialect.
Must go now – Cleo's come my way,
and 4er oik dfcf mnj.

Marie-Lynn Hammond did a song on this same subject, "Keyboard Kitty," on her CD *Pegasus*. There is also software available that will detect cat-like typing and lock your keyboard.

Enjoy!

*M*y girl and I, we went one day
to an all-you-can-enjoy buffet.
We could enjoy our choice of drink –
coffee, tea, or juice, I think.
The smorgasbord had a deployment
of condiments "for your enjoyment":
enjoy some butter on your muffin,
enjoy your turkey with some stuffin',
enjoy your salad with some dressing…
all enjoyed with placards' blessing:
"Enjoy a little or a lot";
"Enjoy this carefully – it's hot."
When seated by our server boy,
we were commanded thus: "Enjoy!"
When he came back, after a bit:
"How are you enjoying it?"
I thought, when we had had our fill,
he'd ask us to enjoy our bill!
I asked my girl, when she was full,
if she'd found it enjoyable.
She said, "Well, you know what they say:
You can lead a horse to a buffet,
but you can't make the beast enjoy it –
if you push, you'll just annoy it."

Does the overuse of **enjoy** bother you as much as it does me? Some people seem to believe that using it in place of "eat," "drink," etc., puts the addressee in a more positive state of mind. But enjoyment is a subjective experience, and cannot be commanded any more than one may order a person to fall in love.

Some antics of semantics

a response to a usage in some school math texts
I'd like to have words with the rubes
who write "4-sided number cubes."
What next? A twenty-sided sphere?
Obtuse right angles? Should be clear!
Perhaps we should, in English class,
let "noun-verb adjectival" pass.
In physics class and research articles
we might as well allow sound particles,
and get the kids in shop to make
a fast-accelerating brake.
Perhaps the staff room now has got
tequila in the coffee pot!
These butt-head word-wreckers can't stay.
To fix the problem, we should pay
these writers of semantic wrecks
with quarter-one-cent-loonie cheques.

Some parents object to dice – "Instruments of the devil! Tools of gambling!"
So the schools, to keep things from getting too dicey, call them **number cubes**
(since they don't want to just avoid using them at all). But, even given the
dodgy justification for that, since when is it responsible in a school text to
refer to something that's not a cube as a cube? If it's four-sided, obviously it's a
tetrahedron. Well, some textbooks use such things as **4-sided number cubes**.
Yes, it's been seen in the wild. I kid you not.

A plurality of options

If I were moose, I don't know what I'd do –
I wouldn't know if I were one or two.
I'd have a condundrum if I were deer;
I wouldn't know if I had a dear deer, I fear.
If I were coupled, to be elk would be bad...
But the truth is I'm not; I'm just single and sad.
To be multitude or to be one and only...
at least I could pretend that I'm not lonely.
Ah, yes, I could dream that I had my wish
when introducing myself as "fish."
My singleton state would surely be hid
as long as I was shad or squid.
And if someone would take me for what I am,
we could be two groupers, as happy as clam!

English used to have several classes of nouns, and some of them didn't change in the plural (some also underwent changes to the vowel, not all of which have been retained in modern English). Now it has normal nouns and "irregular" nouns. Some languages get by without marking the plural at all, though... context can be relied on quite a bit.

Violent types

*I'*m concerned; I can't stay silent:
typography is just too violent.
I've just seen an altercation
over marks of punctuation.
One guy pulled a † out,
slashed it in the air about;
‡s soon clashed in
there to ™s on the skin,
/ and \; the correction
was ÷ dis§;
then, with iron |s aswing,
these two £ed everything.
By °s this awful ruction
led to µtual destruction:
neither fighter being swayed,
with two •s points were made.
What's to do? How many ×
must we countenance such crimes?
I just don't know what to think;
I've no ¥ for spilling ink.

Here's a translation:
I'm concerned; I can't stay silent:
typography is just too violent.
I've just seen an altercation
over marks of punctuation.
One guy pulled a dagger out,
slashed it in the air about;
double daggers soon clashed in
there to trademarks on the skin,
slash and backslash; the correction
was divided by dissection;
then, with iron bars aswing,
these two pounded everything.
By degrees this awful ruction
led to mutual destruction:
neither fighter being swayed,
with two bullets points were made.
What's to do? How many times
must we countenance such crimes?
I just don't know what to think;
I've no yen for spilling ink.

X-rated! (not for sensitive eyes)

A little Latin loving

I met a pretty dancer, ca.
midnight, fresh from a mazurka.
I asked the girl if I could get her a
drink, some ice, a kiss, etc.
She said she had no time (i.e.,
she had no time to spend with me).
I made more plain my assets, viz.,
that I was in the language biz,
and offered her some perks, e.g.,
a fast tongue and some poetry.
She was impressed. She made a call
and soon was joined by friends et al.
I found words thrilled her quite a bit.
I got to know her friends (op. cit.).
We wagged our tongues all night. P.S.
Does that mean what you think? Oh, yes.

This one's trickier. The abbreviations of Latin terms are to be pronounced as we normally would when seeing them on the page: some as the full word, others as the letters. So the expected pronunciation is in bold, and the meaning is in parentheses: ca. = **circa** (about the time of), etc. = **et cetera** (and more), **i.e.** = id est (that is), **viz.** = videlicet (namely), **e.g.** = exempli gratia (for example), **et al.** = et alia (and others), **op cit.** = opere citato (in the work cited), **P.S.** = postscriptum (postscript, addendum).

Prelude to an unexpected weekend at the estate

To an estate I've been invited.
The lady has me quite excited.
To England I've not been before,
but listen up to what's in store:
she asked, "Do say, may I depend
on you to come at the weak end?"
And in her eyes I saw a gleam.
"We'll have some syrup and I scream.
I hope that you and I may sup.
Just pop on by and knock me up."
I told her I would do my best.
Ah, hospitality! I'm impressed!

The British put the emphasis on different places in some compounds than Americans and Canadians do: **week**end rather than **week**end, **ice** *cream* rather than *ice* **cream**. They also use some different idioms, for example **knock me up** meaning "knock on my door" rather than "get me pregnant."

Ready, hot and bothered

I met a girl who was very sweet,
with a pretty complexion, peaches and cream;
I took her for an ice cream treat
covered with berries, peaches, and cream.

She was very girly, to tell the truth:
all blushes and giggles, sugar and spice;
she also had a real sweet tooth
and ate nothing but starches, sugar, and spice.

She dressed quite well in a girlish way,
and her hair was done up, nice and neat;
she was also organized, I would say –
in sum, she was pretty, nice, and neat.

She was fun, and so I saw her again,
and we dated a while, off and on;
I found she was moody now and then –
her switch was "crazy, off, and on."

Ere long, she said, "I'm realizing
I need some loving, slap and tickle."
Here sense of loving was surprising:
she liked to scratch, bite, slap, and tickle.

For an adventure or a disaster
she was ready, bound and set;
she tied me up and got some plaster,
and I was stripped, cast, bound, and set.

By then, I didn't know what to call it –
it wasn't penny ante, nickel and dime;
she cut up my clothes and emptied my wallet,
every last quarter, nickel, and dime.

The girl I'd dated had transformed –
black and white, night and day –
but I found to her wildness I had warmed
while tied up for an evening, night, and day.

And so it came that we were married,
made man and wife, ball and chain,
and over the threshold she was carried...
along with my shackle, ball, and chain.

She's a devil by night and an angel by day,
crimson and clover, leather and lace;
I live for the times she wants to play
and gets out the vinyl, leather, and lace.

It's optional to put a comma before "and" in a series of three or more items, just as long as you're consistent with it. It can have advantages, though it may seem less casual. This usage is called the serial comma. I was originally thinking of doing something on a serial killer, but the slasher poem was gruesome enough...

A sound thrashing

I know that you're wondering, chickadee,
just what in the world has injured me.
Well, I met a girl who was sizzling hot
who said she didn't get out a lot.
At a glance, my heart went va-va-voom,
and we sped off on her scooter (vroom!).
Squealing round a corner, I lost my grip
on an article of her clothing (slip!).
My head connected with a phone box (ding!)
but I kept with my ride and managed to cling.
We had some trouble with a bird (flap, splat!)
and got scratched up (yow!) while dodging a cat;
she skidded into her doorway with a knock,
but when we went in, I was able to walk.
The marble floors were fresh with wax,
and I slipped some in my sock feet (smax!).
While were were climbing the stairs towards bed,
a low-set sconce bonked on my head.
She fixed me a Scotch on the rocks (clink, clink)
and slipped on a silk kimono (slink!),
and as I gave my Scotch a sip
I felt the crack! of leather whip.
"Now get undressed!" she barked. "Let's play!"
With shears, she snipped my clothes away,
and then my naked buttocks felt
the slap of a hand to raise a welt.
The sum of what filled the following hour
would tax an onomatopoeist's power:
crackle, groan, clank, smooch, slither, wheeze, creak,
thud, moan, crinkle, squeal, sigh, grunt, squeak...
But the sound that made my toe hair curly
was her gasp and cry, "My husband's home early!"
The back door opened and closed (creak, bang);
my heart stopped and my jaw dropped (clang!).

I jumped up to escape my fate
and was grabbing my shreds when she screamed, "Wait!
It's cool! No need to turn and run!
A threesome is his kind of fun!"
I should have stayed, you might assert,
but I was worried that I'd get hurt.
I tore from the room to get away,
and that's why I'm limping so today:
I slid down the banister, like a fool,
and was stopped by the post at the end (Newell!).

OK, I'm playing a bit fast and loose with onomatopoeia (creation of words in imitation of sounds). Some of these are reasonably well established as expressions of sounds; some are inventions; a couple are regular words pressed into service to play sounds that they sound like: **slink** – well, a kimono is slinky, even if the sound it makes when slipping off isn't exactly that – and **Newell**, pronounced "nool," like the sound you might make when your midsection hits the post at the end of a banister... a Newell post.

Indecent prepositions

I met a buxom grammatician
and said I'd like her out to take;
back she came with proposition:
in let's stay and out let's make.

I proceeded with elation
her proposal up to take,
and so prepared my habitation –
out put cat, up bed did make.

In she came and, around stalking,
switfly over she did take
and declared, with eyebrow cocking,
that me over she would make.

Up she tied me then and there
and smoothly off my clothes did take
and while I lay with syntax bare
she with my wallet off did make.

The upshot of my disquisition?
It is how down not to be shaken:
accept indecent preposition
and you might well in be taken.

There is a common belief that it is an error to end a sentence with a preposition. This is another one of those silly ideas foisted upon our language on the basis of Latin grammar. It was popularized by the late 17th-century dramatist John Dryden and the 18th-century Oxford professor of poetry (and Anglican bishop) Robert Lowth, neither of whom knew how English works nearly as well as he thought he did. Like the "split infinitive" inanity, this "rule" has been ignored by good writers over the centuries and is not considered a rule by authoritative usage manuals. It should go without saying that we don't want to put prepositions *too* far away from the verbs they pair with, but one might hope we can exercise sensible judgment. This poem was inspired by this "rule," though it does seem to have gotten away a bit... for one thing, some of the prepositions in it are actually adverbial uses. Nonetheless, I think it illustrates reasonably well the hazards of always putting the preposition before the verb to avoid ending the sentence with it.

The elements of lust

I met a chemist just by chance
in the Pd at a dance.
I'm a bit of a B the dancing floor,
so I thought I'd try a little more.
I asked, "Would it be much amiss
to lead a Rn your mouth with a little kiss?"
She said, "Oh, please, don't get me wrong.
It's just – your W inches long."
"I know," I said. "It's fun for play,
though when I it's in the way."
She said, "Then let's be somewhat bolder,
with my right Ne your left shoulder.
The days Ar when I would shy –
they're dead; let's Ba, say bye-bye."
My sense of shame I'd S a Ni,
so we commenced some slap and tickle,
but even I turn Cd red
to think of where our actions Pb...
The host told us we had to stop or
we'd be dragged off by a Cu;
it took some Au to Fe it out.
But this adventure left no doubt:
in love, I'm not so sentimental...
I'll take a girl who's elemental.

The various chemical symbols, which have to be pronounced as the full name of the element, are: Pd = palladium, B = boron, Rn = radon, W = tungsten, I = iodine, Ne = neon, Ar = argon, Ba = barium, S = sulfur, Ni = nickel, Cd = cadmium, Pb = lead, Cu = copper, Au = gold, Fe = iron. Note that the I in line 10 is iodine, not simply the first-person singular pronoun. Cadmium red is a bright red.

Love's letter's lost

I have a letter from my beau;
the prospect sets me all aglow.
Though by his spoken words I'm smitten,
I've never read a thing he's written.
What does it say? "I hope your well" –
He talks of plumbing? What the hell?
"Your in my thought's and in my dream's."
He's missing words here, so it seems.
"Although your butt apart from me
a little while seems large." I see!
My lover measures my behind!
"All ass, all lack!" Say, do you mind?
Well, then, what else? "If I we're there" –
well, I'm not with you anywhere –
"I'd give you Rose's." Rose's what?
To hell with her, the little slut!
"I'd give you lovely Violet's two…"
OK, you jerk, that's it. We're through.
"However we are now apart,
so I shall stay – helled in your heart."
At least you got that right! "Good buy!"
He takes me for a hooker! Fie!
Well, I will bid this lout "so long"…
in speech, so right; in print, so wrong.

How many relationships founder on refusal to accommodate the other's faults,
orthographical or otherwise…

Sweet lies? Sweet lays?

He: "Will you not with me ally?"
She: "Will you now my doubts allay?"
He: "I'm in earnest – would I lie?"
She: "I'm for Earnest – would you lay?"
He: "I'm not used to that reply!"
She: "Could you use a quick replay?"
He: "On your words can I rely?"
She: "These are words you can relay."
He: "You sound smooth, but you might fly."
She: "You feel smooth, and I might flay."
He: "You with looks your words belie."
She: "You with words your looks belay."
He: "You are out to be too sly."
She: "I am out tonight to slay."
He: "With some liquor may I ply?"
She: "Will you lick her? You may play."

Anyone who hasn't been harangued at some time or another on the distinction between **lie** (intransitive, what you do when you horizontalize your body) and **lay** (transitive, meaning to cause another person or thing to lie, or, colloquially, intransitive, meaning to lie with another person, so to speak), please raise your hand. No hands? Everyone's heard it? Marvellous. And yet **lay** has been used to mean **lie** since the 14th century, and was quite commonly used thus in the 17th and 18th centuries. Perhaps this is because it really is a causative formed on the basis of the past-tense form of **lie**. Or perhaps the distinction isn't a very important one for many people.

That indirect object of desire

I met a salesgirl in a store
who said that she could sell me more,
but when she had all I could give her,
I found she'd sold me down the river.
How I got taken there's no doubt:
she said that she would take me out.
"I'll get you lunch – I really should!"
She got me lunch? She got me good!
She bought me... she bought me a drink;
I swallowed it, hook, line, and sink.
She took me home and, like a flirt,
said "Come, I'll fix you some dessert."
I didn't know, in my delight,
that I would soon be fixed, alright.
She squeezed me, then squeezed me a lime,
and said "I'll give you quite the time."
She tied me up, whipped me some cream –
and then she whipped me, made me scream.
She crushed me while she crushed me grapes...
and then her friends parted the drapes.
She made me food, made me a mess,
made me a toy, to my distress.
Tossed me a salad, yes she did,
and then they tossed me like a lid –
flipped me while flipping me the bird.
I'll leave out all that next occurred.
At last they left me, left me money,
left me spinning – thought it funny.
She'd offered me some fun; I bit;
she offered me for fun. That's it.
I'm wishing now that I'd thought twice,
and so I'll give you some advice:

when choosing objects of attraction,
pay attention to the action;
if your object's too direct,
you might not get what you expect.

Some verbs can take in indirect object – a recipient of the action – or not.
English happens to use the same form of the pronoun for indirect objects
as for direct ones. This is one of the things that make it so much fun. The **me**
that doesn't change between **squeeze me** and **squeeze me a lime** (the latter
meaning "squeeze a lime for me") in German is **mich** in one case and **mir** in
the other. Where's the fun in that? We used to have that kind of distinction in
English, too. Good thing we got rid of it.

R-rated (adult, but not quite as sizzling)

A miss-calculation

*O*n Valentimes, I wrote a note
to a lovely lady – let me quote:

O, how many × must I declare
none = my loved one anywhere?
Her beauty is > any you'll find;
she's no < perfect in form and mind.
It's me + her through the ages sublime;
we shan't be ÷ nature or time.
My beautiful number passes the test;
of all the world's loves, – the best.

I held my breath, and, by and by,
my declaration got this reply:

Dear sir, in spite of all you're implying,
we will in no times be multiplying.
Your little additions subtract from the tone;
we should be divided and left alone.
Your words hyperbolic are too exponential;
the sense and the real are at differential.
Your planned integration is rather fanatical;
to get to the root, it's simply too radical.
Though you're positive a fair answer is waiting,
I'm negative – your love is too calculating.

How could I have misestimated so?
I know not how to transform my woe.
I've lost the apple of my i,
a prime little number as sweet as pi.
Derivative words won't open her door...
or leave her alge-bra on the floor.

OK, I confess. This isn't really about language usage. It's a bunch of math puns.
But even mathematical signs are forms of language.

To sweetly split the infinitive

A fetching young virginitive
sought out a buff grammarian
both lusty and contrarian
to split her sweet infinitive.

She said, "Please do it neatly –
I'm sure 'tis not a sin
to slip an adverb in
to split an infinitive sweetly."

He asked, "Where would I fit it?
It seems an imposition
'twixt verb and preposition."
But she asked him sweetly to split it

before her mood had passed,
"for all the best writers do it."
So together they went to it
to sweetly split it at last!

The "split infinitive" is a favourite bugbear of prescriptivists and is something that probably most people "know" is an "error." However, there's no basis for this belief in English history and usage, and current authoritative usage manuals generally assert that the "rule" against it is not a rule at all. You may even occasionally read that it's actually impossible: although we're in the habit of treating the "to" in, for instance, "to do" as part of the infinitive, it's not an indispensable part of it – we all *should to have noticed* that it doesn't go with the infinitive everywhere. And "splitting the infinitive" is often the most straightforward, elegant, or plain old clear way of phrasing something, as many of the best and most revered writers of English have known over the centuries. It also allows extra nuance, for example the difference between "really to do something" and "to really do something." The supposed rule was invented on the basis of Latin grammar. Latin doesn't split its infinitives. Well, of course it doesn't! They're one word! And what has Latin to do with English? Julius Caesar didn't wear pants, but that doesn't mean you shouldn't.

BUT TO NOT
WEAR PANTS IS
IN FASHION,
BARBARIANS.

A parenthesis

*P*arentheses: cradled hands holding your message,
neatly bestowing a soft little blessage
(so much more peaceful than the visual rackets
that may be created by using square brackets).
They're a velvet ink bag to soften hard words
(or a little surprise gift, loaded with turds).
Say your friend (a co-worker) sends you an email
suggesting (or foisting) an unattached female –
a little blind date (or myopic at best)
who's eager to meet you (or willing when pressed).
Are you free (it's been set up) on Friday at 9?
You can meet (if she shows) at the Savoy to dine.
She's heard all about you (it goes without saying)
and she says you sound nice (she's been told that you're paying).
So you put on your suit (Goodwill, $10.98)
and comb down your hair (not much work) for your date.
She's awaiting, with perfume (or bug spray) anointed,
and she seems quite demure (probably disappointed).
You order some drinks (loosen up things a notch);
her tastes are refined (she takes single-malt Scotch).
You make conversation (one word at a time);
you find she's quite eloquent (just like a mime).
You think that she's pretty (the drink's kicking in),
and she smiles dreamily (she has moved on to gin).
The food comes (at last) and it's simply divine
(like food offered to gods – burnt and sprinkled with wine).
Your date has filet mignon (charcoal briquette);
you went for the chicken (to stay out of debt).
For dessert, it's Napoleon (from water loo)
and the chef's special (leftover) tiramisù.
The mood is romantic: you look in her eyes
(or, anyway, somewhere 'twixt forehead and thighs).
You feel that she's warmed to you during the meal
(it's the closeness that comes from a mutual ordeal).

You call for the cheque and slap down your gold card
(two full meals and twelve drinks, tax and tip, damn that's hard).
You offer to walk her home (can't hurt to try);
she accepts (she's afraid she'll fall over, that's why).
When you get to her door, you make as to kiss
but she blushes and turns (she's afraid she would miss).
But the evening ends well – witness plans that you make
to talk in the morning (she'll nudge you awake).
Ah, parentheses – they let you keep your composure
and charm (while still offering total disclosure).

Note that a parenthetical comment should be able to be removed from
a sentence and leave it intact, coherent, and properly punctuated (if less
interesting).

Conditioned response

*O*ne winter eve I chanced to meet
a lassie who was very sweet.
I felt a rather quick attraction,
though she measured her reaction.
I asked her, "Would you like a drink?"
"I would, but I'd best not, I think."
"Then could you join me for a dance?"
"I could, but I can't take the chance."
"Perhaps you'd like to sit and chat?"
"I would; I do; so let's do that."
We passed a pleasant hour or so
until she said she had to go.
I had some thought of what to do:
"If you would like, I'll walk with you."
"I would like – on a second date,
but not a first; you'll have to wait."
"Well, could I get your number, then?"
"You could if I but had a pen."
I gave her one; she said, "I can.
Now here it is. Do use it, man."
I must say, I did not expect
one so demure to be direct.
Next day I got her on the line:
"Hi! Would you like to come and dine?"
"Would I? Please tell me the condition
governing the proposition."
"It's at my place. I cook, you eat."
"You've found my style. When shall we meet?"
And so she came, I cooked, she ate,
and as we talked, and it grew late,
I gained a gradual suspicion
her parries were not inhibition.
I tested whether I was right:
"Say, would you like to spend the night?"

"I would," she said, and closed to kill:
"However. Ask me if I will."
"Do stay. Now, will you?" You can guess
to this she said a simple "Yes."
It seems she's not a girl who warms
to indirect politeness forms!
Since then, we two have been together,
all the time, in any whether.
I mince no words positionally;
she loves me unconditionally.

It's quite common to use indirect forms, asking about the possibility of things rather than making direct requests. This allows deniability on the part of the person asked without apparently rejecting a direct request, avoids sounding too importunate, and allows the requester to pretend that a rejection was not a rejection of a direct request. It's face-saving all around. These forms are proof that we cannot ignore the pragmatics of speech; attention only to the literal denotative meaning often overlooks the entire point of the communication. I'd have to say a girl would really have to be very attractive for a guy to overlook such literal-minded pigheadedness as we see above – but maybe she was just playing a game.

Abso-freaking-lutely!

*M*y girlfriend had some words with me. It seems she's walking out,
and her excla-screaming-mations left the reason in no doubt:
"I'm abso-freaking-lutely tired of all your stupid crap.
I thought you were Prince Charming; well, you're a-jerk-nother chap.
You think you're empe-lording-ror of my exist-damn-stence.
Well, I've got infor-spitting-mation, buster: get thee hence!
Your lack of spic-and-spanness has me in di-screaming-stress;
I'm sick and puking tired of your for-endless-ever mess.
You phil-all-screwing-anderer, your eye will always roam,
yet your expec-snatching-tation is that I'll stay barefoot home.
Well, you will see tail chasing will just bite you in the end:
I'm leaving now to go see my new boy-believe-it-friend.
You look quite non-dumb-plussed. You find my words a little strange?
I'm inde-flying-pendent, bud, and that ain't gonna change."
I wasn't much sur-jumping-prised to learn she felt that way,
just taken quite aback she had the tmesis so to say!

Yes, there's a word for when you stick one word in the middle of another, as
in **absofreakinglutely**. It's tmesis (not to be mistaken for temerity). It goes
without saying that it's normally used just for the insertion of expletives. Most
of the instances you see above are, shall we say, unattested.

Some linguists call this process infixing. Infixing is like prefixing or suffixing,
only instead of adding an extra bit of a word before (prefix, un+happy →
unhappy) or after (suffix, freak+ing → freaking), it adds it in the middle. This
is a common process in other languages. The thing is, though, fixes – prefixes,
suffixes, and infixes – are bound morphemes; they can't stand on their own.
Tmesis is the insertion of whole independent words.

Persuasion and conviction

I met a fetching lass pedantic.
Conversation turned romantic.
I was eager; she was warming
to the bond between us forming.
Virtuoso-like she played me:
"Please convince me and persuade me."

Gamely I set out my reason,
naming assets, citing season,
speaking to the sense refined.
Word by word I turned her mind,
but her body shied, evasive:
"Quite convincing; not persuasive."

So my talk turned to her beauty,
called her hormones to their duty,
eyes a-gazing, stroking hand –
she could not the urge withstand,
but her thoughts recoiled. She winced.
"I'm persuaded... not convinced."

Then I spoke of words and passion,
matching tongue with her in fashion,
showing that a fine distinction
may lead sense into extinction,
matching lip to lip the while
so to thought and sense beguile,
till our wills were one unaided,
both convinced and, yes, persuaded.

The formal distinction (for those who maintain one) is that when you convince someone, you change their mind, whereas when you persuade someone, you get them to do something. Many will, on the basis of that, say that one ought not to speak of convincing someone to do something - persuading them to do it, yes, or convincing them that it's worth doing, but not convincing them to do it. Some people are quite passionate about this distinction. Many others are entirely unaware of it and cannot be convinced to maintain it.

An abbreviated romance

*Y*ou Ave. girl, your heart's desire;
you met her in your church Esq.
one pretty summer eve in Jun.
and dated her by lt. of moon.

You Rd. with her across a pond
and Dr. somewhere back beyond…
Your lady is the tippling sort;
get to the Pt., get out the Pt.

But take the Hwy.? I've Sr. kind:
you Ct. with one thing on your mind.
Oh, when with beauty you acquaint,
the time for modesty this St.

You know in Jr. heart's a lark –
you'll stay in the Pkwy. after dark,
but it's the Pvt. things you'll do
that will have Maj. dreams come true.

But when she's flown off in Sept.,
will you have Mr.? Will you remember?
She Mrs. you, but you've moved on…
you were her K; she was your P.

The various abbreviations stand for the following words, the pronunciation (not the sense) of which is necessary: Ave. = avenue, Esq. = esquire, Jun. = June, lt. = light (not Lt. = Lieutenant), Rd. = road, Dr. = doctor, Pt. = point, Pt. = port (hee hee… gotcha), Hwy. = highway, Sr. = senior, Ct. = court, St. = saint, Jr. = junior, Pkwy. = parkway, Pvt. = private, Maj. = major, Sept. = September, Mr. = mister, Mrs. = missus, K = king, P = pawn.

Mark the lovers

*W*hen a lover after dark
Requests a little court and spark
And love-ee, after some digestion,
Makes a note of the suggestion,
She uses a question
mark!

When your love is more than lark,
You vow to board the wedding barque,
And signify your great elation
At impending conjugation
With exclamation
mark!

When in passion you are stark
And lover's name in throes you bark
But say it wrong (you'll blame congestion)
The "Oh" that meets your indiscrestion
Will have a question
mark!

When quiescent neighbours hark
To domestic spat and snark,
If they transcribe the situation,
What signifies a protestation?
An exclamation
mark!

But what if you could combine them? Read on...

Where is the interrobang?!

*W*hat's up with English punctuations?!
Usually we have a glut,
but for certain situations,
we don't have a mark?! Say what?!

Just how can we express the fate,
the dread, the voices overwrought,
when boyfriend says to girl, "You're late?!" –
when girlfriend says to doc, "I'm what?!"

What signifies the threat to life,
the terror felt and burden carried,
when man looks up and says, "My wife?!"
and mistress says to man, "You're married?!"

That feeling that you're going to hang,
you're screwed, you're done, you're wrecked, you're toast...
interrobang, interrobang,
where are you when we need you most?!

The interrobang (from **interrogative** – for the question mark – and **bang** – a typesetting term for an exclamation mark) was first proposed as a single punctuation mark in 1962 by ad man Martin K. Speckter and was available in fonts by 1966. But, while it had a brief minor vogue, it didn't really catch on. You can find it in some type faces on your computer now if you know where to look, however. Thus, the premise of this poem isn't *quite* true – the interrobang does exist. So why don't we use it?

A slightly extreme story

I fell just a bit for a girl
who was moderately unique:
her beauty was slightly stunning,
her body was somewhat sleek,

her mind was to some degree brilliant,
her wit to a measure unfazing;
she was also a bit like a tigress –
in bed she was mildly amazing.

I ought to have known our romance
would cause the stars nearly to cross,
for she was somewhat the daughter
of the guy who was kind of my boss.

Her father was more-or-less adamant
that our joining was sort of forbidden,
but we were both kind of in love,
so we carried on pretty much hidden.

But it all fell a little to pieces
when we saw where our romance had led,
for she was increasingly pregnant...
and I was increasingly dead.

The boss was a bit apoplectic
when he heard of what had transpired;
he lightly turned eight kinds of purple,
and I was, in general, fired.

I was almost dazed, just a bit bankrupt,
but left the truth nearly unspoken
that I was to some extent terrified
my heart would be left slightly broken.

But I felt a little astonished
to see what my love did for me:
she declared, so to speak, to her father
that she'd marry me to a degree.

She found herself loosely disowned,
but we generally went our own way,
and we sort of have something you might call
a happy small family today.

Of course, deliberate understatement for comic effect is always available. But there are some terms that are by nature rather extreme or even absolute. Some that are generally thought of as being so are gradually coming to be used in less absolute ways – **unique** is everyone's favourite example. Is "more unique" wrong? Some will tell you that it can be read as meaning "more in the direction of unique" or "closer to unique." I think that **unique** here is actually being used to mean **unusual** while keeping the "interesting" tone of **unique** rather than the "odd" tone of **unusual**. Well, but is it wrong? Hmm. Well, if it is at all now, it probably won't be within a few decades. It's passing into acceptance. And so it goes. Words shift meanings all the time. **Nice** used to mean "foolish," for instance. You can do your bit to resist a change that you don't want to see happen. Who knows? You might even succeed. Wouldn't that be nice?

They did it

*I*t started late that evening when Barney said to Gord
he wasn't getting younger and his wife was looking bored –
he made her the suggestion they should have a little fun,
and when she told her counterpart, the playing was begun.
Marica said to Vicky that she ought to drink some more,
and when she took her glass she took her husband to the floor.
They danced a little waltz and then they did a little fling,
and when the song was over they were game for anything.
The two that were not dancing met each other by the bar
and they talked and then she said "I wonder where the others are."
He looked and saw them dancing and he thought they'd join the game,
and so he took her by the hand and they both did the same.
They danced around each other in big circles on the floor
and they swung and reconfigured from the way they'd been before.
And then they parted from the crowd, propriety forgetting,
and found a shady nook where they could do some heavy petting.
Things went from there and such it was that, at the morning light,
Marica, Gord and Vicky said 'twas like no other night,
and Barney, more pedantic, when he wrote of it at last,
saw no clear antecedents for the evening that had passed.

Every third-person pronoun – **he, she, they, it** – needs an antecedent, a noun
specifying exactly *who* this he, she, they, or it is. Sometimes, though, there's
more than one possible candidate. Careful writers do well to watch out for this
– and either avoid it or, as serves their ends, exploit it.

Who sent the percent

I sure do wonder what he meant,
the guy who drew the first %.
Was his intention to disguise
a cubist nose and pair of eyes
that evermore would look askance:
"30%? Ha! Not a chance!"
Or was it drawn at first to show
you use it when you say o-o:
"What sort of portion is enough?
80? Oh-oh!" That kind of stuff.
Or maybe it should be a set
of tennis racquets and a net:
"Your share is 40 – will that do?"
"Percent? No, 60!" Back to you.
It doesn't take an intellectual
to see this sign as vaguely sexual:
"What's that dick offering? Oh, that's rude!
Just 45%? You're screwed!"
I might descry, if I may dare,
a Z with curlers in its hair,
a slash with earrings, or an S
that's cut in two and in distress,
but at last the thought it brings
is of a pair of wedding rings,
therewith a line the twain dividing
neatly drawn and so deciding
some for him and some for her.
With this in mind, I might aver
the man who started this mark's journey
was not designer but attorney!

There's also a per-thousand (per mille) sign: ‰. And, yes, one for per-ten-thousand (which I guess one could call per myriad; doesn't matter, I've never seen it outside of my computer's character palette): ‰o.

My veil of tears

*O*h, woeth me! I've fallen hard,
hosted by my own petard!
In one fowl swoop, my just desserts
have been served up – and, boy, it hurts!
I have betrayed my love, but plead
compulsion by deep-seeded need!
Whole-scale short-sided wrecklessness
has got me in an awful mess.
My Jane was straight-laced; I was cursed,
chalk-full of need to slack my thirst.
Although our lives were going fine,
I just couldn't tow the line.
When on a small site-seeing tour,
I took a pretty southmore's lure:
jar-dropping beauty, looks to kill –
with baited breath I stood stalk still.
"I have a view that's quite unique,"
she said. "Let's go and sneak a peak."
Why did I heed her beckon call?
Free reign of passions leads to fall,
but what I thought led straight to hell:
"She'll tie me over – my as well!"
We didn't buy our time that night;
we cut straight to the cheese on sight –
I won't mix words: our will to dare
just grew like top seed then and there.
As if possessed of slight of hand,
in never regions we did land
(to name a view would be too course
and put the cat before the horse).
When all was done, I had the sense
I'd face cognitive dissidence,
but thought I'd pawn off bold-faced lies.
At last I had to realize
my power mower was not one-of
when I got news that caused my love –
a note a few months later: "Soon your
southmore will produce a junior."
I got a mindgrain; I could see
a storm in the offering for me.
My Jane was cued in, bye and bye,
and she raised up a human cry
in a high dungeon. "You've done wrongs!

Let's go at it, hammer and thongs!
The chickens have come home to roast!
I won't lie doormat now! Your toast!"
She caused a raucous with abuse
and anger I could not diffuse.
Her words were nasty – so profound,
my vocal chords can't make the sound.
She was a bowl in a china shop,
beyond the pail. I said, "Please stop!
The dye is cast! It's not the place
to cut off your nose despite your face!
Don't get your nipples in a twist!
You give me short shift! I insist
I'm utterly beyond approach!
Don't treat me like a mere cockroach!"
She cried, "My cause for consternation
is not a pigment of the imagination!
There's a bi-product of your lust!
Get out! You fill me with disgust!"
The point was mute; my chance was past,
so I gave up the goat at last.
Fate accompli, forgotten conclusion –
my morays were my dissolution.
And so, without further adieu,
here's some advice that's trite and true:
It would be who of you to trust your gut;
nip wayward passions in the butt.
Don't sow your wild oaks around –
the eggcorns might just bring you down.

An **eggcorn** is a misconstrual of a word or phrase on the basis of an inaccurate (but seemingly sensible) analysis of its parts or origins. It uses other existing words or word parts in place of the originals. The term **eggcorn** is of course one such – the word should be **acorn**. The six dozen eggcorns in this poem have all been observed "in the wild" – used by real people in earnest, not as jokes (see eggcorns.lascribe.net). The eggcorns (and their proper forms) are **veil of tears** (vale of tears), **woeth me** (woe is me), **hosted by my own petard** (hoist with my own petard), **one fowl swoop** (one fell swoop), **just desserts** (just deserts), **deep-seeded** (deep-seated), **whole-scale** (wholesale), **short-sided** (short-sighted), **wrecklessness** (recklessness), **straight-laced** (strait-laced), **chalk-full** (chock full), **slack my thirst** (slake my thirst), **tow the line** (toe the line), **site-seeing** (sightseeing), **southmore** (sophomore), **jar-dropping** (jaw-dropping), **baited breath** (bated breath), **stalk still** (stock still), **sneak a peak** (sneak a peek), **beckon call** (beck and call), **free reign** (free rein), **tie me over** (tide me over), **my as well** (might as well), **buy our time** (bide our time), **cut to the cheese** (cut to the chase), **mix words** (mince words), **grew like top seed** (grew like Topsy), **slight of hand** (sleight of hand), **never regions** (nether regions), **to name a view** (to name a few), **course** (coarse), **put the cat before the horse** (put the cart before the horse), **cognitive dissidence** (cognitive dissonance), **pawn off** (palm off), **bold-faced lies** (bald-faced lies), **power mower** (paramour), **one-of** (one-off), **caused** (cost), **mindgrain** (migraine), **in the offering** (in the offing), **cued in** (clued in), **bye and bye** (by and by), **human cry** (hue and cry), **high dungeon** (high dudgeon), **hammer and thongs** (hammer and tongs), **come home to roast** (come home to roost), **lie doormat** (lie dormant), **your toast** (you're toast), **a raucous** (a ruckus), **diffuse** (defuse), **profound** (profane), **vocal chords** (vocal cords), **bowl in a china shop** (bull in a china shop), **beyond the pail** (beyond the pale), **the dye is cast** (the die is cast), **cut off your nose despite your face** (cut off your nose to spite your face), **don't get your nipples in a twist** (don't get your knickers in a twist), **short shift** (short shrift), **beyond approach** (beyond reproach), **a pigment of the imagination** (a figment of the imagination), **bi-product** (by-product), **the point was mute** (the point was moot), **gave up the goat** (gave up the ghost), **fate accompli** (fait accompli), **forgotten conclusion** (foregone conclusion), **morays** (mores), **without further adieu** (without further ado), **trite and true** (tried and true), **be who of you** (behoove you), **nip in the butt** (nip in the bud), **sow your wild oaks** (sow your wild oats), and of course **eggcorns** (acorns).

A form of love

$\mathcal{D}$ear [name here], I just want to say
I'm glad we met on [insert day].
To see you at [location here]
was something I'll hold ever dear.
Your [colour] eyes and [colour] hair
trump any I've seen anywhere.
To talk with you on [insert theme] –
my favourite subject – was a dream.
[If dining is involved:] The food
was [well/not] suited to the mood,
but I could hardly taste a bite,
you filled me with such keen delight.
[If dancing is involved:] Your grace
transported me to outer space;
I never thought I'd have the chance
to fly to heaven with a [dance].
The fine caress of your sweet hand
was almost more than I could stand,
and then I tasted rapture's bliss
when, at [time here], I dared a kiss.
That was the gate to Xanadu,
and when it opened, we leapt through.
On [fabric] sheets, we knew delight
such as I've felt no other night.
When morning came, and we did part,
[name here], it nearly broke my heart.
I know I've found the love I seek –
this shaft from Cupid was unique.
I hope you'll see my words are true;
[nickname], I could love none but you.

This last one's just for you.
